The Redundancy of Tautology

Leilanie Stewart

Dedicated to Joe and Keanu,

who are with me on the road less travelled.

Acknowledgements are due to the editors of the following magazines: *Decanto, Sarasvati, Weyfarers, Erbacce, Neon Highway, The Blue Hour, The Sound of Poetry Review, Mudjob, Boyslut,The Journal, Dead Snakes, Lagan Online's Four X Four magazine and Poetry Scotland's The Open Mouse* for previously publishing some of the poems in this collection.

Contents

Ripe Fruit

Will I ever grow up?
The vine says no
Which vine?
Not the grape vine-
the vine with spreading lianas
the vine delving into
the depths of a slumbering
consciousness

Why bother growing up?
When the acrid clouds are waiting…

It is better to stay
young and unplucked
free of herbicide,
free of pesticide,

hanging on the vine.

Carefree

The curtain
ripples on the breeze
oblivious to the tables
of people worrying
about debt

and the jazz plays
as if to serenade
the curtain,
while it floats
on an azure sea,
somewhere,
in a place
I know nowt of

but here,
now,
life goes on…

Times tables

Twelve times twelve
is a hundred and forty,
the number you aim to reach
at the end of your multiplications,
and hence graduate
from primary school.

A hundred and forty
was the weight
of a perfect martial artist.

English Litter-ature

A long time ago
I hoping to remember this
therefore, and but,
I'm gerund out of here

Does this poem annoy you?
Do you find that I'm not
a very inarticulamate person?

I'll have you no
my degree is first crass
from Oxbridge.

Portaheater

What a bunch of crap-
day in and day out
and yet
the green paint flakes
revealing
the faded,
watermarked,
flowery wallpaper beneath
on the remnants of a wall
where cockchafers
chased
henchafers

Can't you imagine
the segments
sequentially
fragmenting
the fragility
of a yestcrycar
that was one dark
tar pit
although
there's poetic beauty
in even the deepest
darkest
depths
and what do we do
with crude oil?

Let the fires burn!

Twenty two ways to cook and serve a fish

Boil it
Fry it
Grill it
Sauté it
Roast it with tomatoes
Make it into fish parcels
Serve it with parsley sauce
Try your hand at goujons
(if you know what the hell they are)

That was only eight things
you'll note if you can count-
the others are up to your imagination

There are plenty of fish in the sea
but make sure you avoid
the kind that sting,
the puffer-fish with poison
the ones who eat meat
Foolish you for thinking
we apes had the upper hand
we may be top of the food chain
but the cartilaginous ones
of the deep Triassic
would eat us whole,
bones and all

Silly fleshy people.

The Opposite of White is Black

The lighthouse
has had enough
of sharing light with ships
that would be better off
crashing against the rocks,
sinking into a stygian abyss,
simply because
they carry cargo from
one port to another
and never question
their orders.

Standing on a lone promontory
the lighthouse knows
erosion will soon cut it off
The fog will roll in, surround it,
on its limestone stack.

Tomorrow will not be the same
but that's ok
life is better for the lighthouse
in the dark; tainted,
than on an easy ride
over a glassy bay.

Underdog

Take a running jump
and dive into the swamp,
do them all a favour,
turn yourself overnight
from an underdog
to a martyr
before they make
a scapegoat out of you,
string you up by the hind legs,
flay your hide,
tan it in the sun
and turn you into a duffel coat.

Optical Illusion

The two lines
are the same length
but one has inverted arrows
at either end
and the other
has everted arrows
giving the illusion
that it is in fact longer

The four by four
black dots
on a white page
look like an ordinary grid
until
you shut your eyes
and see grey dots
in between

Are you any superior
to the seemingly poor bastard
standing next to you?

Pointless

Why does she sit
with her legs dangling
over the side of the bed?
Contemplating,
the world
Pondering,
every last detail
of her life,
incessantly.
Yet it all amounts
to nothing
When it's put
in the great spectrum
of all things;
the wheel that churns out
every android
that ever was.

Don't shoot him next to the drinking water

What is this?
I'm reading and I'm actually starting
to enjoy the rhythm, syntax,
then I stumble upon a seed:

•

Not a seed, a hole,
a cigarette burn
or not, since there aren't
any charred edges

It's a shape, a sphere
marring the surface of my mind

This page is white
stare at it for a while
and you'll see the veins
of the bloated dead body
encompassing it

The bleach wasn't used
to make the pages any less caustic

The black shape is a fake elixir,
imperfect opal - there are flaws
Don't bite: Warning
there may be lead bits in it.

Friendship for the cynical

It might look like
the biggest gold nugget
you've ever clapped eyes on,
but in actual fact
it's an aluminium tube
that's been painted with a copper tint
and hollow on the inside.

Fold-up box

How does one fight
when one is naked?
when one has nothing
to pull out of one's sleeve
and defend oneself with?

If you go into a shop
and look for a box,
your eyes scour the room
for a three dimensional object
with six sides

But if the box is flat
you won't see it at all,
and this feeling is exacerbated
if you find out that
you were in the box to start with

Metamalfunction

You can talk
about this
and this
and this
but not that

You can talk
in dark
shady
corners
of the mind

We can talk
in dark
shady
pubs

We can talk
about anything,
everything,
except that <u>one</u> thing-
not <u>*that*</u>

Implosion imminent
in five,
four,
three,

two,
one,

pop-
fizzle.

Brown Envelope

Leilanie Stewart
Interpretation House
Meandi Road
Utopia
UR1 2ME
Dear Editor,

I am a brown envelope in a sea of brown envelopes. I am a tiny brown envelope floating on the sea of possibilities. Scoop me from the slush pile with your net. Read me, love me, want me. I am a tiny envelope on a big desk, not a big envelope on a tiny desk, but I wouldn't have it any other way. For you see, when the waves are bigger, I can get carried further. So far, this meandering river has taken me to the estuary, and now I feel the strong tide sweeping me away. Don't let the riptide pull me to the bottom. Give me a chance to float into open waters, let me drift across the ocean into a land of sunny horizons.

Yours Faithfully,
Leilanie Stewart

Glass Vision

The glass is breaking
can't you hear it?
How can you deny it?
when the wind enters freely

The glass was perfect
pristine and smooth
not a blemish to mar the surface
an immaculate face to the world

The glass was always there; me and it
not for a moment did I take it for granted
yet I envied its strength and purity
a sycophant's desire

Now the glass is broken; the view has altered
No longer will I look through the same window
although the frame
will always be the same.

Inspected and void

My kettle is full
of corral
and ammonites
I wouldn't be telling you this
if the wool wasn't clogging my ears
and the steam
clouding my vision
you can think me insane if you wish
I'll help you stop speculating
and confirm what
you already conjectured-

this world suffers from mass schizophrenia
there are few of us who walk alone,
sober amidst the hysteria.

A Fat Load of Wadding

Hanging draperies,
tapestries,
yards and yards
of fabricated fabric,
all made in a
man-machine;
not a man-made machine,
but one where fingers
worked like spiders
skittering over looms,
weaving
faster, faster
Arachne!
Arachne!
Don't break the thread
or we'll all go spinning into
mortal disambiguation.

Idle

Brain to glutes
Twitch. Move.
don't wanna
don't need to

And to my head?
My fibula
fibuling

Brain to finger
a flicker
a tricker
It started there…

Leg over
Leg over
the willing, but

a moment surrendered
thought lost in time.

Landmass

There is a lone   stack
standing out at sea,   a sad
promontory that's   jutting
beyond the riptides.   I often
watch it and wonder   why
there's only one,   because,
surely if it was formed   by erosion
there'd be more along   the coast
This is a desolate beach   to walk along
and when I go there by   myself, I try to
imagine that under the   surface of the water
the cliff and the stack are touching, holding
onto one another through the swells, and
though the peaks and troughs will do their
damage, what is under the surface will
never be erased, and never be separated.

Tick the right box

I'm not white
Backwards and forwards: one dimension
I'm not black
Left and right: two dimensions
I'm not brown
Up and down: three dimensions
Am I yellow?
But what is the fourth dimension?
I'm not red
Travel through time: fourth dimension
I am mixed
The fourth dimension
is only science-fiction.

The devilry of spastic colon

Spastic bowel slithering
rippling
inside, intestines contract
effervescent.

Oesophagus floodgates
opening
flowing, calicum carbonate runs
benevolent.

Convex stomach
shuddering,
burning, pyloric sphincter made
efflorescent.

Distended gut is
churning,
quieting, gastric reflux tsunami
imminent.

Nautical Almanac

Watch me move my leguminous feet,
wriggle my toes into the earth
and see how the bacteria fix

nitrogen

which travels on a tidal surge
from nodule of root to acetate heart
then transpires through my aquiline core

not far from where I am.

Robotomy

You could
armour plate yourself,
weld
metal chips
the whole length of your body,
slowly fuse yourself
into a man-machine.
I could program you then
with all that I ever
envisioned you could do
but you never did.
You could be the robot,
in the human,
that never malfunctioned.

A Flash in the Pan

Wouldn't it be nice
to burn bright, hot,
with ferocious intensity
then extinguish with a bang?

Wouldn't it be better
than burning long, slow, giving off
meager heat and light?

But what if the firecracker
had a faulty fuse, instilled
by an inadequate craftsman;
a product of a futile society?

Firecracker will sizzle, spit
and burn,
but the smell will linger
long after the firecracker has gone

Whichever way you will have it
make sure to leave a scorch mark
in the middle of the floor,

for others to follow.

Crater

When the soul is pock-marked
it is probably best
to fill in the holes
with *Polyfilla*, or
some other type of grout,
you see,
it's never good to show any gaps
if you want the mosaic
to look complete,
and all that really matters
in society today
is how it all comes together
on the surface.

Eternity in a chasm

Aphrodite in the hypogeum cocked her head to the side
her tenebrous prison; fit for a goddess?

Surely not. Eons in earth unclothed and alone
curves far removed from fantasy, admired by Hades. But

only once had spade touched stone
and rubble rained on stygian purity.

Above, seven cows stood shoulder to shoulder
watching the humans toil and sweat.

So that was death for an idol of old?
They understood well for science killed truth.

Devolution

If there is an imbalance
that must be corrected
for one to be centred
one has to devalue
the corrosive feelings

Those are the feelings
that eat at the core of being,
erode a person from inside out,
starting in childhood

See this poem?
See how it is detached?
the impersonal nature
is for the best

For to go out, guns blazing
is counterintuitive.
Remember that the body and mind
are both physical;

The snakes won't go away easily-
they have to be driven out.

Free of free radicals

When you put
zinc oxide on
it's thick and chalky
so it sits on your skin
as a layer,
not becoming absorbed
into your body

This is the kind
of symbiotic relationship
that we, as humans have
with our food
and with the weather

Some kinds of pets
make mutual companions
without drawing out
more from you
than you gain from them

At all costs
you must avoid
the psychic vampires-
charms will not ward them off,
cream will not be a barrier,
but rather a lubricant
protecting your skin
from friction,
making sure
you don't get blisters.

Half Empty

And while
there is breath
in your lungs
and warm blood
in your veins
you keep on swimming

For a corpse
may have its last
exhalation
as the plasma coagulates
in its concrete limbs

And you may say
it all stops, but surely,
life is better than that

The stream
will not carry this one
off the tower block
of existence.

The Hole of Truth

What's behind the ferns?
With their five pointed hands
And the dense jungle mists
of yesteryear

Through the grey pencil lines
That depress the thick foam
I can see past the leaves
between five points

What's behind the ferns?
Through the veins of the leaves
Past the cracked plaster board
and the finger marks.

Atrophy

I am not a sea cucumber
but I am filled with air bladders

The air bladders make me float
on through the haze of this city

The air bladders help me
to keep my head above the water

in this sea of cucumbers…
in this sea of commuters…

The red balloon came out of nowhere
The red balloon sailed through the air

It doesn't have air bladders
but it floats

The hands came from either side
like the foam on a wave

Like the foam on a wave
they toss the balloon as easily as sea spray

As easily as a sea cucumber

But I am not a sea cucumber

The balloon bounces across the wake
The balloon zigzags over the sea

A renewed sense of hope ensues-
perhaps humanity is not all bad

Perhaps I with my air bladders
am not so different

Maybe I could fit in
as much as an air-filled bladder,
air-filled piece of seaweed

As much as a piece of seaweed
would fit in on an ocean of ~~sparkles~~
~~dreams.~~ ~~hopes~~.

The balloon floats to the ground
The hands have abandoned it
A foot comes out of the abyss
and stomps down

The balloon pops.

A knife in the back

Why
are all the knives
in the sink
when we ate Chinese
with plastic forks
for dinner
last night?

There are gremlins
at work here-
this really pisses me off
to no end!

It's a Metaphor for Something Else

In order to wash your hands
first you must acknowledge
that the tap must be turned on
as nothing other than running water
will wash material objects clean

Then you must wet your hands
and apply soap, rubbing vigorously
until your fingers are covered
in a rich, bubbly lather;
you must get into every crevice
or the germs will breed and multiply

Do not let the germs take hold!
This is a warning - they're dangerous!
Attack them all with malediction
you have no time to worry about others
the bacteria they carry is their own problem.

Perception as Truth

What if the sky was made of papier mâché
and the land a giant bathtub
with its stopper in New Zealand?

And what if the lines of latitude
were rings of wire suspending the paper dome
above the earth?

What if it's all illusion and we're simply make believe
and our eyes are telling us
what they perceive to be the truth?

What does it really matter?
Why do we even care?

Tribulations

She reached down
and pulled off his stamen
carelessly,
like any idle child
tearing the legs
off a fly

He needed his stamen,
unlike a lizard,
able to shed its tail
since he can't grow
another stamen
so readily

Nothing
can be done about her.
People gossip
about her 'condition',
whispering in sheltered corners
talking of trepanning

No amount
of hole drilling in her skull
would alleviate this rose
of the thorns
hand reared by
mother nature

In an age of technology
she's plain and simply
not user-friendly.

Talent

It got darker while I was writing this
Don't you hate it when it does that?
Don't you hate how the birds fly south
and yet we can't

Let's all get jealous of the birds
Let's throw stones at them
all because they have an inborn ability;
They can fly

They get fed without earning money,
without doing a single damn thing
that we must do
in our ornithologically-challenged lives.

Wasp in autumn

I hit it
Squashed it flat against the window
With Decanto
Ah, Decanto!
Unfortunate that I chose the zine
that didn't give my poem a misprint
to read on the morning
when the fly landed…

I slammed
It smeared
It stained my only copy-
Damn!

It could've been one of the others
that put typos in my published poems

And now,
the guy across the aisle from me looks wary
I won't be faulted for my Kung fu reflexes

And the lady in the seat behind is smiling, perhaps,
because she's Chinese, or probably
because she knows I saved us all
from anaphylactic shock.

Verity

Psyche got punished
for wanting to know the truth,
wanting to see the face of her husband

She was banished from the Kingdom
the moment she held
a candle and knife over Cupid's head

It's always been the same, ages before, ages since
that we should live our lives in blissful denial
accepting the hell imposed on us as a slice of heaven

But not me. I'm with Psyche
climbing that mountain to fill her urn
with the purest water coming straight from source.

A change in dynamics

These ball bearings
are made of steel,
but once upon a time
they were made of bath gel,
a long time ago
I could've thrown them into water
and watched them dissolve
leaving beautifully scented foam
and only a slight scum
for residue.

Blood of the Hare

Fear was the bite of the snake
The bite of the snake
That bit me
The hair of the dog
That bit me
Like the hare that I was…
A timid, tame hare

I could've bitten the snake
But instead I bit the bite
Removing a chunk of flesh
And poison from within

I stuffed the open wound
With a handful of foam peanuts
That quickly absorbed the mess
When the blood flowed freely
The polystyrene soaked it up,
Sucked it up,

Remove the symptoms,
conceal the source
of the problem.

Wasp Waist

The woman on the right
has a fringe on her boots
and the woman on the left
has a fringe on her bag
and the woman on the right
has a fringe on her coat
but the woman on the left
has no fringe on her hair
though what the woman
on the right doesn't know
is that the woman
on the left
can lure the bees
away from the honeysuckle
with her chocolate.

Death of Narcissus

The shed was always there,
a faithful old friend
and yet the years went by with reality unchecked;

it used to be one sheet, but now
the timber is divided

As each season passes,
creosote determines
its resistance to the elements

If you look at the grain, it's permeated
with fine veins of character
This shed has seen a lot in its noble lifetime,

though as I sit, now
transcending tête-à-tête
stripped bare; futility looms.
Where charm dies,

acceptance is a narrow passage of hope.

Appreciation of the finer things in life

They float on by in a haze of acrylic
I wonder if they feel emotion
jutting proudly, but standing alone
how nice it would be, to feel so brave

There's always a cost, a price to pay
if you don't sieve quickly, it'll catch up with you
for we're all mortal, and they're included
not one of us can mess with time

Don't tell me that's the way of things
I don't believe in destiny
Things get frustrating in the material plane
but on the slipway, existence detaches

Twice or thrice?
It's all invented
Just sit back and laugh
At least that's my opinion

Still, they came before us
And I'm jealous, I admit it
though it's foolish to cry
takes mind over matter to conquer.

Melifluous Inclinations

They're lined up in rows
Immaculate. Pristine. Clean.
I could go on with a bunch of adjectives,
but I'd be digressing from the issue;
all I see are obstacles,
hurdles,
to jump over
making my ankles catch,
making me trip.

I don't want to fall,
prefer not to crash and burn
I want a smooth path
though I know
life doesn't always give us
what we desire.

Live wire, Earth wire

It's shaped like a cylinder
with a triangular spout at one side
and a curving handle at the other
you call it a kettle

Attached to the kettle
is a long plastic cord
that conceals wires inside
attached to a plug

Pick up the plug,
it's plastic too. Now see the three prongs?
Stick those into the wall
where you'll see three holes

The holes are square
one on top, two below,
put your plug in those holes
and push the button

The button is in the socket,
it's a switch, if you like,
and if you follow all these steps
you'll never receive an electric shock

Conform.

Coma

As I lie here
in this vegetative state
dictating to myself
in my head, I realise
there is no true silence
while the flesh is warm.

My mind ticks over
but my body can't keep up
thoughts dissipate
into the ether,
knowing one day my body
will follow.

Until then, I lie
trapped by carbon
my limbs perfectly still
but the metaconscious
racing, the definition
of quiet, is unknown.

Certified Passed

Double oh
nine one
da-de-dah
a bunch of numbers
you get the picture

This machine
has been appliance tested
and passed

Do not remove the sticker-
The sticker displays prestige
like a karate belt

Karate belts are good
at holding up your trousers.

Nip it in the bud

Go ahead
pinch it
put pressure on the tip
with a blue-frosted finger and thumb
be sure to squeeze hard

If you nip it in the bud now
you won't have to do
anything about it later

Isn't it good
to fuel the fire of the idle?

A leaf at a time

Take time
to live for the moment,
appreciate the good things in life-
the blue cloudless sky,
the whisper of wind through the trees,
the bees pollinating the bushes
outside the open window…

Focus on one minute at a time
for soon you could be in the soil outside,
fertilising those bushes
that the bees like to pollinate

And you wonder,
why bother
appreciating the moment
when it all takes a dark turn

So here's the disclaimer:
listen to me
for I have a fever
for life.

Lapis Luzuli

Don't ask me why,
but I hate the word 'lacunae';
it sounds vulgar,
like a derogatory term
for a part of the female anatomy

Now, if I were to decorate
this 'depression', or lacunae
with lapis luzuli, suddenly,
it would be transformed
into a ritual fit for any Pict.

Fiendish Aphorisms

Charm means
you see the devil in life
as your sweetist, bestest friend

Corrosion means
you see that asshole in life
as the person you want to hate
but truth hurts

Truth hurts
because you can't deny facts
and when facts die
(as all things do)
who will live on?

The devil will die
in the minds of simpletons
but the plastic jellyfish
in the Pamela Anderson of matter
are not biodegradable.

Societal Norms

Happily seanile
head spinning,
ears ringing,
for the milk of life,
eyes burning,
for the joy of truth,
focussing
concentrating
on the fluff,
the tufty, pillowy,
fluff

And you thought
you'd ridden
the ride
of clichés
and were enjoying
this safe,
straight-forward poem,
but you didn't like
the fluff

Ha!
The burgundy fluff
is here to stay

What to do, what to do?
Well, it certainly ain't mainstream, baby.
Too bad I'm an asshole,
eh?

Embroidery Soul

The leaves were made of velvet
and the bark of suede and leather
pieces glued together

The leaves were all hand-stitched;
sewn on one by one
with loving care

She watched from her ivory tower,
wondering,
how long it would take

for the seams to come apart
and the craftsmanship to drift
back into the forgotten void

from whence it came.

Black Moth Fluttering

We are part of this world
We are part of this world like a moth
We are part of this world like a moth
beating its wings against a window
like a moth crashing against a pane
against a pane
pain.

We abide by the rules of nature
Like a moth
Like a black moth fluttering
in the corner of a room
The moth that brings misfortune
and gloom
and despair
to a household.

It is an organism too;
a moth
treat it with respect
bow down to laws that govern it
and govern you

But never give in to
What the moth wants you to be
never give in to the fear
never give the fear

a part of you
You hold the power
the power is in you
the power is in the beating wings.

The laws of the cosmos

My ipad is starting
to malfunction
because it's so cold

My book is going soggy
in the rain

Amidst it all
I can feel my heart
beating fast
to the tempo
of a fever, raging through me

When anything in this universe
falls out of equilibrium
it creates a black hole

The words of a poet
who has nothing to say
float into the nothingness

One
By
One.

A faraday cage will keep you safe

I do not wish to be
yet another rivet
painted into the cast iron girders
sealed for eternity
in a rusty, decrepit
railway fence

The train goes nowhere
but it is better to be on it
than a sleeper under it,
than a fence beside it

Look out the windows
along the way
The journey
is all that matters.

Could somebody remove the crocodile please?

The fucking crocodile
put on my
lime green bike helmet
and escaped
into the ether
on my skateboard
of all things

You'd think
that after putting on
my bike helmet-
going to the trouble
of fastening the strap
and adjusting it
over its ears
that it would've taken
my bike

But no,
it had to be a trendsetter,
fucking crocodile.

Ossifried

Every skeleton
has its closet
but inside the closet
what does the skeleton
hang from?

Is it the rope
that made
the skeleton bestow
his bleached bones
upon us in the first place?

Or the metal hanger
twirling,
idiosyncratically
from the rail?

I envy only
the skeleton's demure frame
as I fry in this heat.

Fuel for a wandering mind

Peter stood next to Mary
on her right hand side
Cathy was opposite Jill
standing next to
the only boy
Two girls stood between
Peter and Jill
And Jill held
onto Dawn's left hand
Between Cathy and Jill
where the Miller twins
and little Tessa
sucking her thumb.
Who was on
Dawn's right hand side?
The mind could go numb
thinking it through
I'd rather think of UFO's
or wonder if Cathy
had ginger hair
and liked to eat porridge
for breakfast.

The Simplicity of All Things Far Away

She said she was going to the shop with me
She was going to the shop with me
She was going, she was going
She was gone. Gone
And yet she wasn't at the shop with me
The door was in front of me
A big oak door with brown and cream
And did I scream?
Hell, yes!
And I banged and banged, but
Still the shop was there
And I was here.

What's really in your drink

There's bound to be wasps inside cans of coke
when you open them up, you can hear them fizz
as they whirl around in aluminium ecstasy
I'm wary when putting a can to my lips

There's probably a drosophila or two in your beer
Flying high on the CO_2
and floating dead on the plethora of bubbles
their carcasses protein for contraband fools.

Bland tasteless junk

I'm trying to like them
no, really
I'm trying
I've even switched pens
to make it look fresh
my opinion, I mean
As I slowly look down
the numbers in the margin
like the steps to hell

Oh damn! There - I said it
I was trying to be positive
Yet I read
and re-read
and imagine, or force
myself to see beauty
when all I can see
is a
pale
    beige
            blancmange.

New-sense

Hair
clings to a shred of scalp

After death,
it is best,
to crush the skull
into bone powder
and fertilise the plants

What a nuisance
a new-sense
of doom

For skeletons
do not keep growing,
their hair
and nails
fall to the whims
of the velvet casket

The four walls
can only contain
what was a foolish
ego
of a myna bird
mimicking,
poorly,
a parrot
in the first place.

Show, not tell

This
grey matter
this ball
of squishy,
squashy,
saturated fat
is oversaturated
with puss and shit

This
sat-upon
oversaturated
shit
holds so much
squishy, squashy
purity,
but the masses
wouldn't comprehend

Misanthropy
it ain't
for if there weren't sheep
the beauty of the shepherd
and the devilry of the wolves
couldn't be appreciated

There hangs
the golden sheep
taunting us so readily

but they are unequipped
with a long enough rod
to reach it

Wield your shepherd's staff!
All you abysmal sheep.
Reach the damn fleece
that you can't see hanging
before your eyes
because of all the glinting gold

What you didn't know
is that the fleece already fell,
cloaking your head
with a suffocating blanket

The blanket
ain't made of wool-
it's polyester,
ha ha!

I warned you
it was filled with puss and shit,
let me remind you-
the grey matter

The grey matter
has been skull-fucked
into a thousand fragments
of anterior cortex,
right hemisphere,
left hemisphere,
leaving only the reptilian brain

A reptilian brain
ain't no good
in the skull of a ram
oozing rotting flesh.

The Vacuum of Innerspace

Give them a bit of love
otherwise
they're just musty, fusty appliances
therefore
they're gathering mould and mildew
furthermore
sitting untouched, unneeded…
sigh!

What's the sense
in being a one-hit
google wonder?

The politics of picking your pants…

…Out of your butt-crack
I mean to say,
who ever told you it's taboo
to do such a thing
in public?

What anally retentive person
invented
such an arbitrary rule?

Aren't we all apes?

Don't we pick our teeth
and scratch our scalps
and

Stop!
Draw a line

––––––––––––––––––––––––––

Poking your nose
and picking your pants
out of your butt-crack
is going too far

You heard me!
Going too far…

Please do not lower the tone
any further

May I remind you
that this
is a civilised
DISCUSSION.

Thou dost protest too much

Scoot over
for the corrugated iron roof
will ultimately fall

See those pigeons?
One-two-three-four
eating their fill-
it will not crash onto them
they will eat, oblivious

Nobody is immune
this is a disaster
that is imminent,
a concrete tsunami
that we may or may not
be able to surf

Prepare yourself
for when the tide turns
people will scatter,
flee in all directions
and what will you do?

Freeze?
Stand and stare?
Self preservation
is of utmost importance.

At age three on a geological timescale

My volcanic-plug head
Sat atop my shoulders
And my shoulders were boulders
Upon a Drumlin torso

And four stacks jutted
From this torso,
The top two giving way
To fingers of spiky tors

At the base of the Drumlin
Where there might have been a spit,
There was instead a lagoon
Oh what I goon I used to be

When I was three.

Snowball Effect

I'd like to introduce you to
Miss Lauren Tide
She came all the way
From Greenland
And is planning to stay
for a while,
an epoch perhaps.

She'll be bringing along with her
Miss Tundra, Miss Glacier
and Mister Permafrost

She was forced to emigrate
from her home, up North,
by convection currents-
hot air brought on by CO2

She'll cool the seas before her,
Push the Gulf Stream further south

It's a waiting game now
for the snowball to come
She'll wipe out the arrogance
of humankind, with one swipe
from her terminal moraine.

A Snapshot in Time

Sunset
on wood; a blood-orange stain
spreading fast, but fingers faster
chasing it across the plains.

Shadows
long but never far
the square is closing: smaller
as leaves roll up behind.

Greyness
looms, a thread of light
on the edge of a precipice
fingers keeping it from the void

Blue
cloaks violet and memory slips
into dark
to chase the sun.

Abstraction

The time of the leaves is over
the leaves are falling
off their tree
they fall alone
sweeping a path
among the other withering souls
spiralling to their demise

A few brave ones
dare to touch each other
knowing it is their autumn
knowing that while
on the surface they care
ultimately it is
a lonely journey.

Blue Light

In a corner of the room
there shines a blue light
the rest of the room
is lit by phosphorescence
yet this light still shines
-blue
the room is windowless
so it isn't apparent
where the blue light comes from
and the room
is not conducive
to a natural brightness
the blue light is serene,
ethereal
but there is no such
otherworldly realm
in this boxed existence
the blue light lingers
never fading
shining down
from a solitary corner.

Sandland

The whiskey burns the throat
like sand in a storm over wasting dunes
and the spiky grass stands to attention
it stands and sways and is shot down
the aggregates are bullets on the breeze

It's a rough old life in Sandland
In Sandland they fall and are forgotten

But the whiskey has lost its medicine
And at night the ears crack
with the bangs and the cries
the roots go deep, but still sand erodes
it can't hold together under assault

It's a rough old life in Sandland
In Sandland they fall, though we try to remember.

Closing time for unwanted souls

The hallways never end
the rooms smell
like chemical loos
the guinea pigs
are eating the carpets,
pulling up the threads,
unravelling the wool

It is all futile;
the cycle will never end

The only way to escape
is to pick any door
take a chance
and run for it.

Long haul

And now
I have a dead left leg
and my belly hurts
and my eyes sting
at the sight
of the see-through knickers
on the line

they're made of net,
what a catch!

Isn't this prison existence wonderful?

Jigsaw puzzle

Just because
the foam jigsaw puzzle
doesn't fit together
doesn't mean
that it's inferior
and even if
the yellow slots awkwardly
against lime green pieces
never meant
to be forced together
in the first place
doesn't mean
you should love it less,
or that
you can find the snake,
but not the ladder.

Look all around you;
at your clipboard
with the metal ring
that doesn't quite
snap neatly into place

Do you discriminate
about everything
in life?

Light at the end of the tunnel

If you didn't know
what your reflection looked like
how would you be able
to recognise your own body
when having
an out of body experience
from a point floating in mid air?

Extra sensory perception
is reserved only
for those with good imagination.

Fodder

It's too late now
there's no going back
It's been ripped out
It's all downhill from here

You should've thought properly
before you let those garish lines
perambulate with spiky heels
across my heart

That which cannot mend itself
is always a slave
listen to the whispers
they're telling you what I can't condone.

The Redundancy of Tautology

If carbonaceous meteors
only contain
5% carbon
then why are they called
carbonaceous?

And if the word crepuscule
means twilight, or dusk
then why not simply say
evening?

This is all counterintuitive
like saying pusillanimous
instead of cowardly

Then again,
if we eliminated all the lions
because we have tigers
there'd be an imbalance
in the ecosystem

Wouldn't there?

Miaow!

Pussy-lani-muss.